THE VICTORIAN PUBLIC SCHOOL

Trevor May

SHIRE PUBLICATIONS

Published in Great Britain in 2011 by Shire Publications Ltd, Midland House, West Way, Botley, Oxford OX2 0PH, United Kingdom.
44-02 23rd Street, Long Island City, NY11101, USA.

E-mail: shire@shirebooks.co.uk   www.shirebooks.co.uk

Every attempt has been made by the Publishers to secure the appropriate permissions for materials reproduced in this book. If there has been any oversight we will be happy to rectify the situation and a written submission should be made to the Publishers.

A CIP catalogue record for this book is available from the British Library.

Shire Library no. 494   •   ISBN-13: 978 0 74780 722 3

Designed by Ken Vail Graphic Design, Cambridge, UK and typeset in Perpetua and Gill Sans.
Printed in China through Worldprint Ltd.

11 12 13 14 15   11 10 9 8 7 6 5 4 3 2

COVER IMAGE
School Yard, Eton, 1852. Coloured lithograph by Percy Skelton. Reproduced by permission of the Provost and Fellows of Eton College.

TITLE PAGE IMAGE
Parian figure, *Young England*, based on a sculpture by George Halse, exhibited at the Royal Academy in 1870. Halse was educated at St Paul's School, and was Chief Clerk of Drummond's Bank, yet managed to be a prolific sculptor. The *Illustrated London News* admired the 'muscularly inclined Christianity' that it claimed to discern in this work.

CONTENTS PAGE IMAGE
A 'hot' or scrum in a game of twenty-two-a-side football at Winchester in the 1830s.

ACKNOWLEDGEMENTS
Peter Ashley, page 26; The Bodleian Library, Oxford, page 14 (top); Bridgeman Art Library, page 18; Charterhouse School, pages 38 (top left), and 45 (bottom); Eton College, cover and pages 39 (bottom left), and 43 (top); Haileybury College, pages 39 (top), 43 (bottom), 44 (top), and 58 (top); Harrow School, page 51 (bottom); Lancing College, page 27; National Portrait Gallery, pages 6 (left), and 57; Oundle School, page 35 (bottom); Queen's Royal Surrey Regimental Museum, Guildford, page 59 (bottom); Spellman Collection, University of Reading, page 49 (top right); Uppingham School, pages 29, and 33 (top); Wellington College, page 40.

Shire Publications is supporting the Woodland Trust, the UK's leading woodland conservation charity, by funding the dedication of trees.

CONTENTS

INTRODUCTION

A T THE BEGINNING of the twenty-first century, over 625,000 children in the United Kingdom were being educated in independent schools. A small proportion of these children attended public schools, although such schools are easier to recognise than they are to define. For convenience, a public school is often defined as one whose headmaster (or, since 1996, headmistress) is a member of what was previously known as the Headmasters' Conference, founded in 1869. Most are boarding schools and all are fee-paying. The popular image is of exclusivity, with pupils housed in ancient buildings, and with hundreds of years of tradition behind them. In fact, the great majority of public schools were either founded or re-founded in the Victorian era. The Clarendon Commission, which reported to Parliament in 1864, concentrated on the nine great public schools (Eton, Winchester, Westminster, Charterhouse, St Paul's, Merchant Taylors', Harrow, Rugby and Shrewsbury), yet already by that date there were others claiming recognition. Some people, especially on the other side of the Atlantic, find it confusing that the most exclusive *private* schools should be described as *public*. In origin, however, they were precisely what the term implies; that is endowed grammar schools, with a charter requiring them to provide a classical education for boys drawn from the general public, in contrast with fee-paying schools run for private profit, or home education with a tutor. How did the public schools come about? What did they have in common? And who, if anyone, was the mainspring behind this kind of schooling, which was such a feature of Victorian and Edwardian England?

In May 1918, just six months before the end of the First World War, Lytton Strachey published *Eminent Victorians*, a collection of four biographical essays on individuals (three men and one woman) who had acquired heroic status in the Victorian era. The woman (Florence Nightingale) lived through the whole of that period, having been born in 1820 and dying in 1910; Cardinal Manning (1807–92) lived through most of it, though the life of General Gordon (1833–85) had been cut short by his murder at Khartoum. However, the third man upon whom Strachey shone his searchlight was hardly

Opposite:
Thomas Hughes, the author of *Tom Brown's Schooldays*, was a lawyer, and, between 1865 and 1874, was a Liberal Member of Parliament. He was a leading Christian Socialist, with wide social and educational interests.

5

a Victorian at all, in a strict sense. Dr Thomas Arnold was born in 1795 and died in 1842, only five years after Victoria came to the throne. How could his inclusion in such a study be justified? The answer is that Arnold was credited not only with the reform of Rugby School, of which he had been Headmaster since 1828, but also with producing the very archetype of the Victorian public school, making it an institution at the heart of Victorian society.

Strachey's book, though little read these days, was an immediate sensation. Older readers looked back to the heyday of Victorian prosperity and idolised the leaders of that period. Young readers blamed those same people for the bloody war that was only just drawing to a close. Biographies had been popular in the nineteenth century, but many were massive works, often running to two volumes, fulsome in praise, but light on criticism. Strachey's essays were short, and probed behind the façade of his subjects. In one sense Strachey helped to broaden the view of Arnold's legacy by stressing the many contributions he made to public life beyond Rugby, but at the same time he questioned Arnold's reputation as a great reforming headmaster.

If Strachey tried to prick the Arnold bubble, it was two other books that had inflated his reputation in the first place. One was a biography, the other a work of fiction. In May 1844, less than two years after Arnold's untimely death, an official biography appeared, containing much of his correspondence. It was written by Arthur Penrhyn Stanley, who for three years from 1831 to 1833 had come directly under the influence of Arnold when he had been a

Below:
Dr Thomas Arnold, Headmaster of Rugby School from 1828 to 1842. He is arguably the best-known of the nineteenth-century public school headmasters.

Below right:
Visitors to the tomb of Dr Arnold in Rugby Chapel, where he regularly preached. Sermons given in public school chapels could be a powerful agent of social control.

prefect and sixth form pupil at Rugby School. Stanley was amongst Arnold's greatest disciples, as was Charles John Vaughan (Stanley's brother-in-law), a fellow pupil at Rugby, and later a reforming headmaster of Harrow School.

After the appearance of Stanley's biography, Arnold was never out of the public eye, and his reputation was further enhanced by the publication of Thomas Hughes's *Tom Brown's Schooldays* in 1857. Hughes was a near contemporary of Stanley at Rugby, and his school story went through fifty-three editions by 1892, and has never been out of print. Tom arrives at Rugby as a shy eleven-year-old. He endures the rigours of fagging and bullying (most notably by the villain Flashman), experiences temptation, comes under Arnold's influence in the school chapel, throws himself wholeheartedly into football and cricket, and emerges a Christian gentleman. *Tom Brown's Schooldays*, read by generations of schoolboys and their parents, did more than anything to create the popular image of Arnold's life at Rugby, and to mould the emerging public schools of mid-Victorian England.

Tom enjoys some domestic comfort with Dr and Mrs Arnold. An illustration from *Tom Brown's Schooldays*.

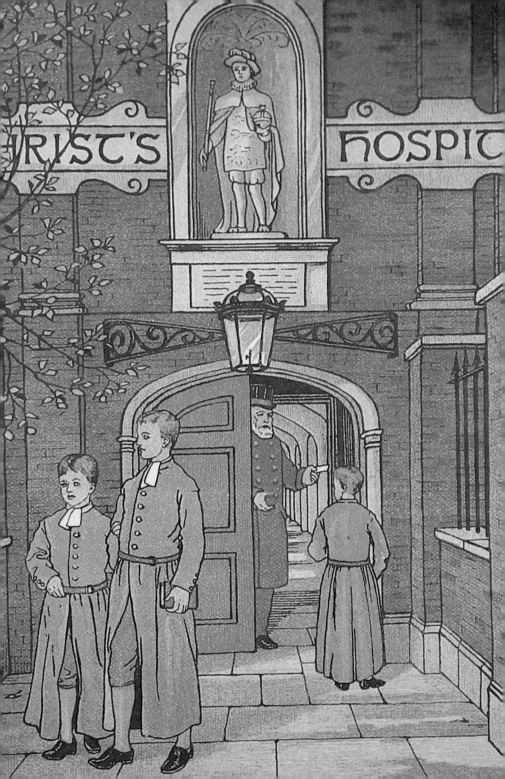

PUBLIC SCHOOLS BEFORE ARNOLD

O F THE NINE public schools investigated by the Clarendon Commission between 1861 and 1864, the oldest foundations were Winchester, which dated from 1382, and Eton, dating from 1440. However, there were much older schools than these, which have since entered the ranks of public schools. The accolade for the oldest goes to King's School, Canterbury, founded around the year 600, making it older than the nation itself. John Mitchinson, its Headmaster in 1869, takes the credit for calling the first meeting of what was to become the Headmasters' Conference.

Although they differed in their precise organisation, all the precursors of the public schools were grammar schools, teaching Latin and Greek, essential to the life of the medieval church, and a prerequisite for entry to the ancient universities of Oxford and Cambridge. William of Wykeham founded Winchester to be in close connection with his other foundation of New College, Oxford. Similarly, the royal foundation of Eton was linked to King's College, Cambridge. These early charitable foundations were not always confined to education. The charter of Eton College, for example, created a corporation to hold property in perpetuity, and to consist of a Provost, ten fellows, four clerks (clergy), six choristers, a schoolmaster, twenty-five poor scholars, and a like number of poor, infirm men. Such diverse aims inevitably left the door open to a conflict of interests when it came to allocating the trust's income.

When John Lyon, a yeoman farmer, re-endowed Harrow School in 1572, he also threw his charitable net wider, making provision for the upkeep of roads between Edgware and Harrow and London. The endowed grammar school that he set up was typical of many at that time, including Rugby School, founded in 1567 by a grocer, Laurence Sheriff. Between the accession of Edward VI in 1537 and the death of Elizabeth I in 1603, some 600 grammar schools in England and Wales were endowed or re-endowed. This great movement aimed to fill the gap left by the Dissolution of the Monasteries and its catastrophic effect on the provision of education by the Church.

Opposite:
Christ's Hospital was founded by Edward VI in 1553, as a hospital for orphans. A school was soon attached in Newgate Street. This illustration from a nineteenth-century children's book shows the traditional uniform of long blue coat and yellow stockings, which, according to tradition, were so coloured in order to keep rats away from their ankles.

9

A Vista View of Harrow, 1845. Nestling beneath St Mary's Church is the original school building of 1615, enlarged in 1819. To the right of the Old Schools can be seen the original school chapel, consecrated in 1839.

The aim of the grammar schools was to provide an education for local boys. A master would be appointed, sometimes assisted by an under master or usher. In return for his stipend, the master would be required to teach, free of charge, the local boys on the foundation. However, sometimes he would be allowed by the charter or the statutes of the school to take in boys from beyond the designated area of the foundation, and teach them for his personal profit. Thus, at Harrow a distinction was drawn between the sons

FOR LONDON AND PROVINCES, 1905-6. 249

King's School, Canterbury, traces its origins to the very birth of Christianity in England. After the Dissolution of the Monasteries, it was reconstituted by Henry VIII in 1541. Advertisement from *Hampton's Scholastic Directory for London & Provinces*, 1905–6.

King's School, Canterbury.

THIS claims to be the oldest Public School in England, founded in the 7th century: reconstituted by Henry VIII. in 1541. The buildings are beautifully situated within the Cathedral precincts and are equipped with all the requirements of Public School life. The Cathedral Choir School is an entirely separate foundation.

The School is richly endowed with Scholarships, Exhibitions, and other Prizes, and has a fine record of Distinctions from the 16th century onwards. Recent Successes (direct from the School) include many Open Scholarships and Exhibitions at the Universities; Admissions to Woolwich, Sandhurst, Cooper's Hill, Indian Police, Naval Engineering College, Naval Assistant Clerkships, Matriculation at London University, etc.

Fifty Foundation Scholarships (£25 to £10), and Entrance Scholarships (£40 to £10), examined for every July and December. Ten Exhibitions, each of £50 for four years, to the Universities, etc. Two are given each Summer.

The Army Class prepares boys for Woolwich, Sandhurst, Indian Police, etc. The Navy Class prepares them for the Naval Entrance Examinations, Admiralty Clerkships, Assistant Naval Clerkships, etc., and the Engineering Class for all branches of Engineering. No extra fee for these Classes.

Junior School, with Scholarships and separate buildings, playground, staff of masters; for boys between 8 and 13.

Excellent health record. Fine historic surroundings. Terms (inclusive): 77 guineas per annum. Junior School: £63 10s.and £70. Numbers,240.

Headmaster   .   -   -   -   Rev. A. J. GALPIN, M.A.
(Late Scholar and Lecturer at Trinity College, Oxford; formerly Housemaster at Marlborough College), with a staff of fourteen Graduates and four other Masters.

Q

In 1509, John Colet, Dean of St Paul's Cathedral, re-founded the school there, using his own money. Somewhat arcanely, his original statutes laid down that the number of pupils should be limited to 153, in reference to the miraculous draught of fishes mentioned in St John's Gospel.

of parishioners, who were to be educated without charge, and 'foreigners', meaning boys from outside the parish. The school lists of Shrewsbury similarly distinguish between local boys and '*alieni*'.

A particularly able headmaster of an endowed grammar school might attract a substantial clientele from beyond the neighbourhood, sometimes drawing them from the entire nation. In such a way did some schools acquire one of the essential characteristics of a public school, namely, that it should serve national rather than local educational needs.

Historically, not all boys had been educated in schools, for home education with a private tutor had been favoured by many of those who could afford it. However, by the late eighteenth century the tide was turning against home schooling for boys (although not for girls). This may partly have been a reflection of demographic trends. With more children surviving infancy, the strain on family life of large numbers of children at home might tip the balance in favour of sending sons (or the most troublesome ones amongst them) away to school. In his biography of Arnold, A. P. Stanley hinted at such a course of events:

> The worse and more troublesome to parents were their sons, the more did a public school seem the precise remedy for them; that the great end of a public school, in short, was to flog their views out of bad boys. Hence…an unfailing supply of vicious sons was secured.

As more sons of the aristocracy entered the public schools, their tone was altered, and not necessarily for the better. With money in their pockets, and little incentive to study in order to earn a living, discipline was imperilled. If parents wanted their boys to be flogged into submission, the schools were prepared to oblige. Indeed, it seemed the only means by which any sort of order could be maintained. That such brutality should have been condoned by parents seems hard to explain, but the half-century before Victoria came to the throne was a period when barbarism was widespread throughout

Charterhouse in 1755. In 1611, Thomas Sutton obtained a royal licence to build, on the grounds of a former Carthusian monastery, a hospital for eighty poor gentlemen, and a school for forty-four poor scholars. The school moved to Godalming in 1872, although the hospital stayed at the London site.

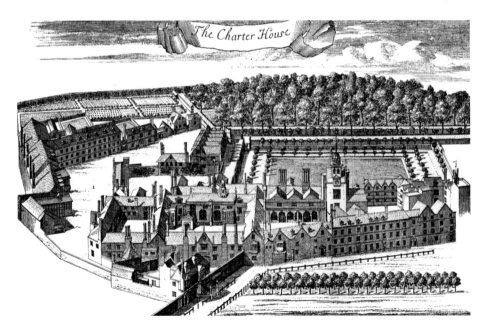

The Charter House

Merchant Taylors' is an example of a school founded by a City company. Dating from 1561, it was originally situated in Suffolk Lane. The premises became increasingly cramped, and in 1875 the school moved to buildings vacated by Charterhouse School. It moved to Northwood, in Middlesex, in 1933.

society, and wantonness and brutality were evident at both ends of the social spectrum. Cruel sports, such as cockfighting and the baiting of bulls, bears and badgers, were popular, and the weakness of the forces of law and order were made up for by brutal punishment, including a legal code which prescribed the death sentence for over two hundred offences. Similar forces were at play in the public schools. For example, it was said of John Foster, Headmaster of Eton from 1765 to 1773, that, being 'unable to control the boys by his personal influence, he had recourse to a system of terrorism, which soon rendered him extremely unpopular'.

Outside the classroom boys were left very much to themselves, and a state akin to warfare existed between staff and pupils. Riots and rebellions

were frequent occurrences. In 1793, three companies of militia were called out to quell a riot at Winchester, and troops with fixed bayonets were there again in 1818, on which occasion a boy had his head cut open by an officer's sword. At Eton in the same year, windows were broken, a wall demolished, and the desk of Dr Keate, the Headmaster, smashed to pieces with a sledgehammer. Keate succeeded in putting the rebellion down, after which he claimed that the boys were 'as quiet as lambs'. Such riotous behaviour eventually died down in all the schools, although Marlborough experienced a serious rebellion as late as 1851.

A schoolmaster, quoted in 1806, gave his opinion that 'the youth of Eton are dissipated gentlemen; those at Westminster dissipated with a little of the blackguard; and those at St Paul's the most depraved of all'. Such views were not unique, and in 1810 an article appeared in the influential *Edinburgh*

Above: The birch was symbolic of the early schoolmaster. This woodcut is from a 1526 edition of *Parvulorum Institutio*, a school textbook written by John Stanbridge, Headmaster of Magdalen College School at Oxford.

Right: The whipping stool at Eton. Engraving from *The Boy's Own Paper*, 1886.

Panel in the Fourth Form of Harrow School, whereon boys (including Byron) have carved their names. There was unrest at Harrow in 1805 and again in 1808; however, the story that Byron dissuaded his school fellows from blowing up the schoolroom, urging the preservation of the carvings, seems to be the stuff of legend.

Review that lambasted the public schools. The author was the Reverend Sydney Smith, wit and controversialist, who later became Canon of St Paul's Cathedral. He had been at Winchester in the 1780s and, though academically successful, hated his experience there so much that, even in old age, the very mention of Winchester made him shudder. He derided the sterility of education in public schools. Schoolmasters, he said, encouraged their pupils to 'love the instrument better than the end – not the luxury which the difficulty encloses, but the difficulty – not the filbert, but the shell – not

15

An engraving by Robert Cruikshank, dated 1826, and entitled *The Tea Pot Row at Harrow, or the Battle of Hog Lane*. Lax discipline at the school at this time gave rise to a number of similar incidents, much to the irritation of local people, but this specific event, if it took place, has not been identified.

what may be read in Greek – but Greek itself'. He had been subjected to much bullying at school, and argued that a boy began as a slave and was likely to end as a tyrant. Public schools, he argued, represented a system of 'premature debauchery that only prevents men from being corrupted by the world by corrupting them before they enter the world'.

Smith had co-founded the *Edinburgh Review* with his friend Henry Brougham, a Scot educated in a Scottish day school, a far cry from the English experience. In 1816, Brougham was elected to the House of Commons, where he succeeded in getting a Select Committee appointed to consider alleged abuses in connection with charities for the education of the poor, which, for historical reasons, included public schools. The Select Committee reported in 1818, and accused Eton and Winchester of deviating from their charters, and of neglecting their poor scholars in favour of the financial interests of the Fellows. A fierce counterattack was mounted and, in order to secure the passage of his Bill to establish a body of regulatory Charity Commissioners, Brougham had to agree to exempt those charities whose charters provided for governors or other overseers. The public schools were let off the hook.

Controversy did not disappear, however, and in the late 1820s and 1830s the number of pupils at many schools began to fall away. Harrow's numbers fell from 295 in 1816 to 128 in 1828. Rugby had 300 pupils in 1821, but only 123 in 1827. At Eton the fall was from 627 in 1833 to 444 two years later. This decline was partly due to a downturn in the economy. It also owed something to the growth of a new religious seriousness (with a strong base in the emerging middle class) in the form of Evangelicalism. Its followers looked askance at the allegations of scandalous behaviour within the public schools. The time was ripe for reform.

Right: Dr Keate, Headmaster of Eton, 1809–34, has gone down in history as a prodigious flogger. He was often the butt of wit: Sir Francis Doyle said of him that 'he had no favourites, and flogged the son of a duke and the son of a grocer with perfect impartiality'.

Below: The village of Harrow was free from suburban encroachment until the latter part of the nineteenth century. The figure on the gravestone is evocative of Lord Byron, who found the tomb of a local man, Peachey, a quiet place for contemplation and composition. The Peachey Stone can still be found in the churchyard.

THE REFORM AND GROWTH OF PUBLIC SCHOOLS

THE DISTINCTION we draw between primary and secondary education is not the same as that which the Victorians drew between elementary and secondary. For us, the distinction is a question of age, with primary and secondary education seen as consecutive stages in a process. For the Victorians, age was immaterial; elementary and secondary education were meant for different *classes* of people. The poor (if they were lucky) received a basic, elementary education, while the middle and upper classes received secondary schooling. Up to the eighteenth century boys were sent away to school at an early age (often eight, although six or even younger was not unknown) and they left at any age, with some hanging around until they were twenty. The problems of such a wide age range are easy to imagine, and the solution was the development of preparatory schools. Amongst the early ones of note were Eagle House, Hammersmith (founded 1820), and Windlesham House (1837). Dr Arnold was anxious to remove boys younger than twelve from Rugby, and he encouraged the efforts of a retired naval officer, Lieutenant C. R. Malden, who established Windlesham House on the Isle of Wight. In the course of time, many preparatory schools forged links with particular public schools, acting as their feeders.

Government grants for the building of elementary schools commenced in 1833, and provision for setting up state-run elementary schools was made in 1870. Very little financial help was given to secondary schools, however, and it was not until after the Education Act of 1902 that any state secondary schools were built. In the free market that existed before that date, the provision of schools for the upper and middle classes was determined by supply and demand, and the prosperity of a school depended on its ability to attract a clientele.

For public schools, demand was growing in the nineteenth century, for industrialisation saw the growth of a large and prosperous middle class. Its boundaries were wide, and included people of enormous wealth as well as those with very little. There were other divides, especially between those whose income came from industry and trade and those who were members

Opposite:
Off to school.
A detail from
William Powell
Frith's *The Railway
Station*, 1862.
Frith used his own
family as models
for this group.
Frith Minor clasps
a new cricket bat,
while Frith Major
looks on with
a marked air
of detached
superiority.

Right: An advertisement from the *St Albans Times*, 1 August 1857, for the Bourne Hall Academy. There were thousands of similar *private* (as distinct from *public*) schools, of varying quality, which provided an education for middle-class boys in the nineteenth century.

Opposite: The bill for William Henry Gunner, a pupil at Winchester College, July 1830. He eventually became Rector of St Swithin's, Winchester, and assistant master and chaplain at the college. At this time, the cost of keeping a boy at Eton or Harrow was around £280 to £320 a year.

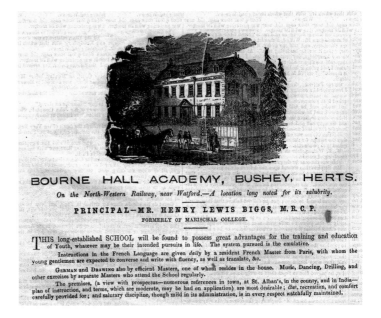

BOURNE HALL ACADEMY, BUSHEY, HERTS.

On the North-Western Railway, near Watford.—A location long noted for its salubrity.

PRINCIPAL—MR. HENRY LEWIS BIGGS, M. R. C. P.

FORMERLY OF MARISCHAL COLLEGE.

THIS long-established SCHOOL will be found to possess great advantages for the training and education of Youth, whatever may be their intended pursuits in life. The system pursued is the emulsive.

Instructions in the French Language are given daily by a resident French Master from Paris, with whom the young gentlemen are expected to converse and write with fluency, as well as translate, &c.

GERMAN and DRAWING also by efficient Masters, one of whom resides in the house. Music, Dancing, Drilling, and other exercises by separate Masters who attend the School regularly.

The premises, (a view with prospectus—numerous references in town, at St. Alban's, in the county, and in India— plan of instruction, and terms, which are moderate, may be had on application) are most desirable; diet, recreation, and comfort carefully provided for; and salutary discipline, though mild in its administration, is in every respect watchfully maintained.

of the rapidly expanding professions. Social status was not accorded to wealth alone. How you acquired it and what you did with it made all the difference. Henry Byerley Thomson made this point in 1857, in his book *The Choice of a Profession*:

> In point of social position the professions have vastly, the superiority over the business world. The man of business has, as a rule, no position in respect of his occupation. If *in society*, his position is the result of his wealth, his education or the accident of his birth, and breeding. He has not gained it by his mercantile pursuits, and he will not lose it should he abandon them. The member of the higher professions on the other hand, at once takes a place in society by virtue of his calling; the poor man of business is nowhere in social position, yet the poor curate is admitted readily to that coveted country society that the millionaire has even to manoeuvre for.

The public schools had limited vocational aims. The sons of the aristocracy did not, for the most part, have to earn their own living; and if they did, they were likely to enter the church or the army – occupations for gentlemen, and in which such training as was necessary was given on the job. It was gentlemen that these schools aimed to turn out. Members of the middle class who were not themselves 'well bred' might hope to turn their sons into gentlemen by sending them to the right schools. The historian Geoffrey Best

Winchester College.

Mr. Gunner's Acc.

	£	s.	d.
Batchelor, Laundress,	3	18	4
Bishop, Hatter,	1	6	6
Bower, Mathematical & Writing Master,			
Corfe, Tailor,	—	12	9
Crutch, Carpenter,	—	5	—
Dear, Bread Butler,	1	16	9
Flight, Glover,	—	5	6
Hopkins, Manciple,	1	9	6
Landy, Barber,	—	14	6
Maskell, Nurse,	—	18	8
Poole, Porter,	—	5	10
Robbins and Wheeler, Booksellers,	7	18	9
Silver, Draper,	—	2	—
Stripp, Smith,	—	2	6
Stubington, Carpenter,	2	4	6
Wells, Beer Butler,		7	—
White, Shoemaker,	2		
Wickham, Surgeon and Apothecary,	1	13	6
Tutors,	+	+	0
Weekly Allowance, for the ensuing Half-Year, at 1s. a Week,			
Money lent for Journey,			
Quarterly Dues, 0 9 3	1	1	3
Bed-Makers, 0 12 0			
	24	9	10
Gratuities, if given,	5	5	0

The Vacation ends on Saturday *Aug: 28*.

The Bread Butler's Bill ought not to exceed the Rate of *21* Pence a Week, nor the Beer Butler's that of *14* Pence

It is requested that no Bills may be paid which are not included in this Account. The Bills are delivered to the Boy, enclosed in a Cover and sealed.

The Money is usually paid to Mr. RIDDING, by the Boy upon his return to College after the Vacation; or it may be paid to Messrs. DEANE and LITTLEHALES, Bankers, Winchester; or to Messrs. WILLIAMS, DEACON, and Co. London, on account of Messrs. DEANE and LITTLEHALES, for Mr. Ridding.

has suggested that Victorian public schools helped define who was, and who was not a gentleman: anyone was a gentleman who had been to a public school or who successfully concealed that he hadn't.'

One of the greatest virtues extolled by the middle class was respectability, a quality quite independent of wealth, and one conspicuously absent from early-nineteenth-century public schools. The schools needed to clean up their act if they were to attract the emergent class. The man the middle class perceived as achieving this task of making the schools respectable was Dr Thomas Arnold.

As was customary at the time, the appointment in December 1827 of a new headmaster for Rugby School was made not by interview but on the strength of the candidate's testimonials, both in number and quality. Arnold's were few in number, but included one from Dr Edward Hawkins, Provost of Oriel College, Oxford, where Arnold had obtained a fellowship in 1815. Hawkins predicted that, if Arnold were elected to the headmastership at Rugby, he would change the face of education all through the public schools of England. Arnold certainly possessed a reformer's zeal. He wrote, 'My love for any place or person, or institution, is exactly the measure of my desire to reform them.' Before he took up his appointment, he wrote to a friend:

> With regard to reforms at Rugby, give me credit, I must beg of you, for a most sincere desire to make it a place of Christian education. At the same time my object will be, if possible, to form Christian men, for Christian boys I can scarcely hope to make; I mean that, from the natural imperfect state of boyhood, they are not susceptible of Christian principles in their full development upon their practice, and I suspect that a low standard of morals in many respects must be tolerated amongst them, as it was on a larger scale in what I consider the boyhood of the human race. But I believe that a great deal may be done, and I should be most unwilling to undertake the business, if I did not trust that much might be done.

Rugby had established itself as one of the leading public schools before Arnold arrived. Dr Thomas James, Headmaster from 1778 to 1794, had raised pupil numbers from 52 to 245, while Dr John Wooll, Arnold's immediate predecessor, rebuilt the school and raised numbers to 381, a number which Arnold never matched in all his years as Headmaster. However, like other schools, Rugby suffered from the malaise of the times, and numbers fell after 1818, dropping to 123 in Wooll's final year.

Arnold took autocratic control of the school, and fiercely defended his independence of the governors. While exerting his own power, he raised the status of his assistant masters by paying them higher salaries and by encouraging them to take in boarders. By this means he intended that they should take greater pastoral care of the boys, while a greater sense of corporate identity would be established. A boy's pride in his 'house' became a cornerstone of the Victorian public school. Arnold rarely acted in matters of discipline without consulting the housemasters, with whom he held regular meetings to discuss school matters. He expected much in return. They were to devote themselves to their school work, and clerical masters (the great majority) were henceforth required to give up salaried curacies in local churches.

There was a ruthless side to his nature. Boys who were considered to be deriving no benefit from the school, or who were doing positive harm, were weeded out. While he used the threat of expulsion freely, there was less recourse to flogging, and repression generally was diminished. He maintained the belief that, in general, boys should be left to govern themselves. 'I cannot remain here', he told the boys on one occasion, 'if all is to be carried on by constraint and force; if I am to be here as a gaoler, I will resign my office at once.'

The Headmaster's house at Harrow, rebuilt after a disastrous fire in 1838. The gradual abolition of dames' houses (boarding houses run by private persons, either male or female), and the taking in of boarders by masters (and sometimes, as here, by the Headmaster himself) helped to build a community spirit in the public schools.

Arnold's observation was an endorsement of government of the boys by the boys. They exercised social control over each other, which allowed headmasters and their staffs to distance themselves from everyday matters of routine and discipline. Boys were very conservative in their rules. Arnold wrote: 'At no place or time of life are people so much the slaves of custom as boys at school.' Customary rules governed many things, including, for example, which items of personal property were considered sacrosanct, and which might be pilfered. The cardinal sin everywhere was sneaking, and it was considered preferable for a boy to lie to a master than to sneak, a view that masters, for the most part, endorsed.

Self-government was to be maintained by a greater use of prefects. The office of prefect or praepostor had long existed, and, in one form or another, was widespread in schools. But Arnold was able to take an existing institution and use it to his own ends. 'You should feel', he charged them, 'like officers in the army or navy where want of moral courage would, indeed, be thought cowardice.' Prefects were to be his non-commissioned officers, acting as channels between him and the boys. Critics argued that too much responsibility was placed upon senior boys, who easily became prigs, a charge often levelled at Arnold himself. Sir Francis Doyle once observed that Dr Keate knew, but Arnold did not, that 'God Almighty's intention [was] that there should exist at a certain time between childhood and manhood, the natural production known as a boy'. Arnold saw everything in terms of a struggle between good and evil, leading Fitzjames Stephen, in the *Edinburgh Review*, to quip that the Rugby boy 'Never ties his shoes without asserting a principle; when he puts on his hat he "founds himself" on an eternal truth.'

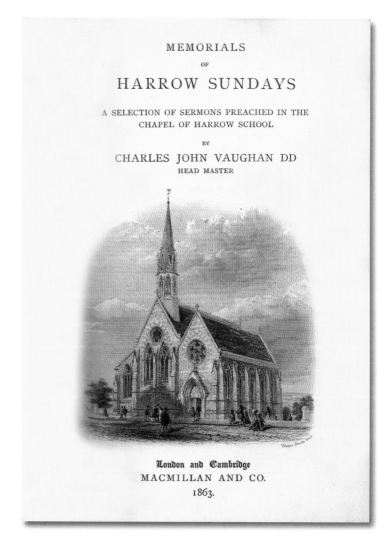

Title page to a volume of Charles Vaughan's sermons, printed after his departure from Harrow. The sermon was a staple vehicle for raising moral tone. The building is the second school chapel, constructed between 1855 and 1861. The spire, which differs from the one actually built, was added in 1865.

MEMORIALS

OF

HARROW SUNDAYS

A SELECTION OF SERMONS PREACHED IN THE
CHAPEL OF HARROW SCHOOL

BY

CHARLES JOHN VAUGHAN DD
HEAD MASTER

London and Cambridge
MACMILLAN AND CO.
1863.

Arnold placed great stress on the chapel, and he insisted that he be allowed to take on the office of School Chaplain when it became vacant. His sermons were simple and direct, and had a great impact on many pupils. It would be a mistake to exaggerate the changes Arnold achieved. As Kathryn Chadwick puts it, 'Before Arnold, public schools were bearpits. After Arnold, they were still bearpits, but with the bears required to put in compulsory attendance at Chapel.'

There were many things that Arnold did *not* do. He did not introduce any new teaching techniques, nor did he widen the curriculum to any great extent. And, contrary to popular belief, and in view of their later significance to public school education, Arnold did nothing to promote games at the school. But what he did do was to restore confidence in the schools generally. As Michael McCrum has said, 'His earnest, high-minded approach appealed to many parents, of both the upper and the new middle class. Thus the children of the old and new ruling groups were intermingled.'

In 1850, *Punch* suggested that learning to read the railway timetable should be introduced into the school curriculum. The spread of the railway network greatly facilitated the sending of boys long distances to a public school.

Charles Vaughan rescued Harrow School from the doldrums in which it had suffered under his predecessor, Dr Christopher Wordsworth, later Bishop of Lincoln. It was not uncommon for clerical headmasters to be offered preferment in the church, an expectation denied to Vaughan after an inappropriate personal relationship with one of his sixth-formers.

Thomas Arnold had many disciples amongst his assistant masters and pupils, who carried the torch of reform to other schools. Foremost amongst these were Charles John Vaughan, educated at Rugby (1829–34) and Headmaster of Harrow between 1844 and 1859; and George Cotton, educated at Winchester, but appointed by Arnold as an assistant master in 1837, remaining at Rugby for fifteen years. In 1852 he became Headmaster of Marlborough, a new foundation, but already one in much need of reform. Vaughan and Cotton share the distinction of bringing organised games into the public schools.

Half of those currently recognised as public schools were founded between 1841, when Cheltenham opened, and 1900. Cheltenham was established on the joint-stock principle. Residents of the town were invited to become shareholders, but were advised that 'no person should be considered eligible who should not be moving in the circle of gentlemen. No retail trader being under any circumstances to be considered.' Marlborough was founded in 1843 as a public school chiefly for the sons of clergymen of the Church of England, many of whom received only modest stipends. Radley followed in 1847; Lancing in 1848; Hurstpierpoint in 1849; Wellington (founded as a national memorial to the Duke of Wellington) in 1859, Clifton and Haileybury in 1862, and Malvern in 1865.

Wellington College, in Berkshire, was established as a national memorial to the Duke of Wellington, who died in 1852.

Not all of the older schools reformed themselves at the same time or to the same degree. At Eton, the relations between the Headmaster and the Provost were crucial, for the one could do little without the agreement of the other. Francis Hodgson, Provost from 1840, enjoyed a good relationship with Edward Hawtrey, Headmaster from 1834 to 1852, and a number of reforms were instituted, both in the curriculum and in the conditions under which the boys lived. The distribution of income between the school and the fellows continued to be a matter of concern, as it was elsewhere. At Winchester, for example, in 1860 the Warden and fellows took for themselves half of the revenues, a sum eight times that paid to the teaching staff at the college. Scathing articles appeared in the press, leading, in the following year, to the establishment of the Clarendon Commission. Its terms of reference were to investigate the finances and management of the nine great schools, and the provision of education within them, but it is indicative of the impact of the new foundations that it also took evidence from Marlborough, Cheltenham and Wellington.

The report proved to be far more favourable to the schools than either critics or supporters had anticipated, and the commissioners recognised the vital role played by the schools:

Lancing College was founded by Nathaniel Woodard in 1848, and was intended for the upper-middle class, whose sons might be expected to go to university. Two other schools, Hurstpierpoint and Ardingly, were intended for lower echelons of that class. Lancing moved to a new, 500-acre site in 1854. The magnificent, cathedral-like chapel was commenced in 1868 but not completed until 1911.

Among the services which they have rendered is undoubtedly to be reckoned the maintenance of classical literature as the staple of English education, a service which far outweighs the error of having clung to these studies too exclusively. A second, and a greater still, is the creation of a system of government and discipline for boys, the excellence of which has been universally recognised, and which is admitted to have been most important in its effects on national character and social life. It is not easy to estimate the degree to which the English people are indebted to these schools for the qualities on which they pique themselves most – for their capacity to govern others and control themselves, their aptitude for combining freedom with order, their public spirit, their vigour and manliness of character, their strong but not slavish respect for public opinion, their love of healthy sports and exercise. These schools have been the chief nurseries of our statesmen; in them, and in schools modelled after them, men of all the various classes that make up English society, destined for every profession and career, have been brought up on a footing of social equality, and have contracted the most enduring friendships, and some of the ruling habits, of their lives; and they have had perhaps the largest share in moulding the character of an English gentleman. The system, like other systems, has had its blots and imperfections; there have been times when it was at once too lax and too severe – severe in its punishments, but lax in superintendence and prevention; it has permitted, if not encouraged, some roughness, tyranny, and licence; but these defects have not seriously marred its wholesome operation, and it appears to have gradually purged itself from them in a remarkable degree.

The Public Schools Act of 1868 was the key piece of legislation facilitating the reform of the schools. At the same time, however, it opened the door to the extinction of the rights of local people to have their sons freely educated as 'foundationers', where such a right existed.

The commissioners recommended that every boy should be taught mathematics, one modern language, and some natural science, as well as drawing and music. They should have a good general knowledge of geography and ancient history, as well as 'some acquaintance' with modern history. The schools were left to introduce these reforms as they saw fit, and the ensuing Public Schools Act of 1868 confined itself largely to reconstituting governing bodies and revising school statutes.

As in the case of earlier reforms, the role of individual headmasters continued to be crucial. Edward Thring (1821–87) was educated at Eton under Keate and Hawtrey. Having taught in an elementary school while a curate in Gloucester, he became convinced that the most skilful teachers were needed for the less able children, and he tried to apply this principle when he became Headmaster of Uppingham between 1853 and 1887. He had no sympathy with Arnold's frequent use of expulsion, and felt instead that every boy had some quality in him, which it was the task of the teacher to draw out. He further differed from Arnold in that he relied less on personal charisma, and more on *system*. He likened his school to a well-run ship that could operate

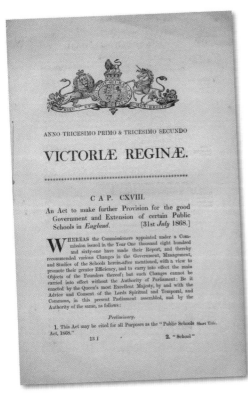

without his presence. Like John Mitchinson, co-founder of the Headmasters' Conference, he did not wish to be 'tied to the chariot wheels of the great schools'. At Uppingham, he introduced much that is now taken for granted, including the gymnasium, the swimming bath, the carpentry shop and the school garden.

F. W. Sanderson, Headmaster of Oundle (1892–1922), was even further from the image of the typical public school headmaster. After attending his village school in County Durham, he became a pupil teacher before proceeding to Durham University, where he gained first class honours in Mathematics and Physical Science. In 1879, he won a mathematical scholarship at Cambridge. Neither a clergyman nor a classicist, he greatly expanded numbers at Oundle, and took the school in new directions, establishing laboratories and engineering workshops. Few public school headmasters took up his enthusiasm for science, believing it less suitable than classics for 'training the mind', and Sanderson's influence is perhaps more to be seen in the new state grammar schools of the twentieth century.

Edward Thring, Headmaster of Uppingham School (1853–87). He turned a small, endowed grammar school into an innovative and successful public school.

TEACHING AND LEARNING

THE HOLD which the classics maintained over the curriculum is reflected in the staff of the public schools. As late as 1914, a list of 114 headmasters revealed 92 to be classicists. Classics masters earned more than teachers of mathematics or foreign languages, and enjoyed a higher status. Ian Hay quipped that it was *de rigeur* to have French taught 'by a foreigner of some kind', but the indifference as to country of origin speaks volumes. At Harrow, the brothers Jacob and Jacques Marillier joined the staff in 1819, the former to teach writing and mathematics (which he did until 1869), the latter to teach French (up to 1839). Of Jacques Marillier, it was said that he lived the life of a dog, and both masters (at least in their early years at the school) were greeted with hallooing and hooting whenever they appeared. In 1855, French was made compulsory for all boys at Harrow. At Eton, mathematics was made part of the regular curriculum in 1851, though it remained a poor relation. Dr Charles Goodford, Headmaster from 1853 to 1862, raised the status of assistants in the mathematical school, who were previously denied the right to wear academic dress. For the first time, some were allowed to keep boarding houses, though without the same disciplinary authority as the regular assistant masters.

The report of the Clarendon Commission was a stimulus to reform of the curriculum, as was the rise of the professions, with more rigid entry requirements. In 1853, the Northcote-Trevelyan Report on the Civil Service noted that 'admission into the Civil Service is…eagerly sought after, but it is for the unambitious, and the indolent or incapable, that it is chiefly desired'. It recommended a unified Civil Service, recruited by competitive examination. Open competition took time to be implemented, but it was laid down for nearly all departments of the home Civil Service in 1870. The purchase of commissions in the army was abolished a year later. Charles Vaughan introduced an Army Class to Harrow in 1851; six years later it contained forty-five boys who received additional instruction in mathematics and 'military science'. A Modern Side was started in 1869. Some of the newer schools set the trend. Cheltenham had a Modern Side from the very

Opposite:
A view of the main teaching room of the Old Schools at Harrow, painted by Augustus Charles Pugin and published by Rudolph Ackermann in 1816. In many schools it was not unusual at this time for multiple classes to be taught in a single schoolroom. Chaos, rather than the order shown here, seems to have been commonplace.

Above: The Lower Schoolroom at Eton. This is the original schoolroom of 1479–88, and remains substantially unchanged, although the appearance of the room was much altered by the addition of wooden pillars in the early seventeenth century. These were needed to support Long Chamber, the dormitory and living space situated above. Notice the open gas burners.

Right:
A Winchester boy at his 'scob', an oak box with a double lid, which acted as a store for books and papers. The origins of the word are unclear. There is a Winchester tradition that it is *box* (or rather *bocks*) spelt backwards, or it may derive from the Latin *scabellum*, meaning a cleric's seat.

Uppingham boys outside their studies, photographed in 1868. Though built by one of Edward Thring's predecessors, he followed the principle of giving every boy a study of his own.

A boy at work in the Lower Schoolroom at Eton. An engraving from *The Boy's Own Paper*, 1886.

A classroom at Westminster at the beginning of the twentieth century. A somewhat posed photograph, with pride of place being given to the phonograph. Educational technology comes to the schools!

beginning, and Marlborough followed suit in 1854. Clifton took a more open view of the curriculum from its earliest days. The competition of new foundations in a competitive market further helped to drag some of the older schools towards curriculum reform.

The prejudice against science remained strong. Rugby was the only school examined by the Clarendon Commission where physical science formed a regular part of the curriculum. Yet Frederick Temple, the Headmaster, in giving evidence to the Commission, observed, 'The real defect of mathematics and physical science as instruments of education is that they have not any tendency to humanise. Such studies do not make a

Harrow boys at 'Bill', a calling over of the roll in the school yard, c. 1910. Such roll calls were a means of keeping track of the boys in their free time. Their frequency varied between schools but, particularly in earlier years, they could be the cause of much friction between masters and boys.

Pupils in the woodwork shop at Harrow, engaged in boatbuilding, c.1910.

man more human, but simply more intelligent.' Sadly, for most boys, the classics hardly made them more human either, as few progressed far enough to reap the rewards of their labours. Edward Lyttleton recalled his days at Eton in the 1880s, claiming that all boys, not only the less able, 'were made to groan and sweat at rudiments, utterly meaningless except as stepping stones to a literature which they never got to read'.

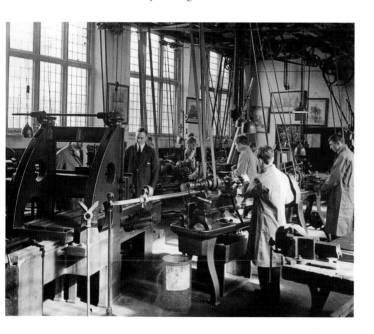

A photograph taken in 1932, but showing the metalwork shops at Oundle School as they were in F. W. Sanderson's time. During the First World War, senior boys spent eight or nine hours a week in the engineering shops, engaged in the manufacture of munitions for the troops.

CHAS. BAKER & CO.'S PRICE LIST.

BOYS' TWEED SUITS.

ETON JACKETS AND VESTS.

For Boys from 9 years of age.

Ready for immediate wear. Thoroughly well cut and made. In Vicunas and Fine Worsted Cloths,

Range 1 ... 17/9 to 25/9
  ,, 2 ... 22/6 to 31/6
  ,, 3 ... 27/6 to 39/6
According to size.

Eton Jackets and Vests to Measure, 21/6 to 27/6, 25/6 to 33/9, &c., according to size.

Patterns Post Free,

HAIR LINE TROUSERS.

For wear with Eton Jackets and Vests.

6/11 to 8/11
8/11 to 10/9
9/11 to 12/11
10/9 to 14/11
11/9 to 16/11

According to size.

YOUTHS' DRESS SUITS.

In fine Black Twills, wit Silk Facing to Jackets.

For Youths from 14 to 1 years,

45/6 to 53/6,

According to size.

THE LIFE OF THE
PUBLIC SCHOOLBOY

THE NEW BOY at a public school had probably formed some idea in his mind, whether accurate or false, of what life for him was going to be like. Perhaps a father, or an older brother or cousin, had told him what to expect, either playing down the terrors or exaggerating them. From the middle of the nineteenth century onwards there was a good chance that he had prepared himself by reading one or more of the scores of school stories that appeared in print. Even so, the reality was likely to be a shock. He was entering a closed community with its own arcane rules and customs. Unlike the world he had come from, it was essentially an all-male society. He would encounter few members of the opposite sex until he returned home in the vacation. When he arrived for the first time, all must have seemed confusion: trails of boys with trunks and boxes, some knowing where they were going; others, like him, completely lost and alone. There was much to learn, and to learn quickly if trouble was to be avoided. Belonging depended on following accepted patterns of behaviour, extending to what you wore, what vocabulary or turn of phrase (often unique to that particular school) you employed, and what deference was to be shown to others, higher up the hierarchy of the schoolboy republic. Only the briefest of settling-in periods would be allowed before sanctions were imposed for breaches of the schoolboy laws.

Although uniform was a comparative latecomer to the schools, certain items of clothing, or manner of wearing one's apparel, had long been either mandatory or forbidden, according to rank and circumstances. Robert Blachford Mansfield (1824–1908), describing the dress at Winchester in the 1830s, wrote, 'Inferiors were never allowed to wear hats inside the College walls; the praefects seldom doffed theirs, except in the presence of a master and when they went to bed.' At Eton in the 1820s, Oppidans (the wealthier boys who lived in the town) wore clothes of all patterns and colours; but Collegers were not allowed to wear trousers. Instead they were required to wear shorts or knickerbockers. Even when this rule was relaxed, the trouser-wearing Colleger would sometimes tuck his trousers into his socks at Absence (roll call) in deference to the rule. When George III died in 1820,

Opposite:
Charles Baker was a major manufacturer of ready-made clothing, and he advertised extensively. This advertisement dates from 1902. Those who could afford it preferred to have their clothes made to measure by a tailor.

Above: Tom Brown embarks for Rugby School by stagecoach. Before the spread of the railways it was difficult to make the start and finish of school terms clear-cut, as boys might be coming and going over several days.

Above right: 'Capping' at Charterhouse was the salute given to a master by touching the back of the neck. It derived from the earlier practice at the school of wearing the cap with the peak at the back.

Right: A Christ's Hospital boy, from *London Visitors*, by James Tissot, c.1874.

Etonians wore black, and when the period of mourning was over, many continued to do so, such that black eventually came to be the uniform colour. Thus, Eton boys of the present day are sometimes said to be still in mourning for the king who had such a fondness for their college.

Bottom Left: Henry Wellesley, later third Duke of Wellington, at Eton in 1863. He wears the cut-away jacket that later took the generic title 'Eton jacket'. This style continues in the military mess jacket.

Below: An advertisement from *Punch*, 1898. The term 'Eton jacket' appears to have been coined at the beginning of the 1880s; 'Eton collar' came into currency towards the end of the decade.

Left: House caps from Haileybury College.

SAMUEL BROTHERS,
LTD.,
65 & 67, LUDGATE HILL, LONDON, E.C.

SCHOOL

OUTFITS

"ETON."
Jacket and Vest for Boy 4 ft. 8 in., 20s. 9d.
Trousers ,, ,, 9s. 3d.
ILLUSTRATED CATALOGUE and PATTERNS free on application.

The introduction
uniform dress came abo
gradually. At Marlboroug
George Bradley succeed
to the headmastership
1858, and, as part of h
attempt to tighten
discipline, set abo
establishing a uniform. H
instructed an Oxford tail
to send down patterns. O
who was present at th
opening of the box
samples recalled, 'Som
fearful suggestions can
out...one we rememb
well as a species of railw

Mr Eve and his
form at Wellington,
photographed in
1861.

guard's cap, with broad red band round the bottom.' It was not adopted. B
at Wellington, around the same time, the dress (designed by Prince Alber
was originally a German-style cadet uniform. This was quietly dropped aft
the Earl of Derby, then Prime Minister, arrived at the station to visit th
school, and handed his ticket to the Head Boy in the mistaken assumption tha
he was a railway official!

At some time during his first day, the new boy would discover where h
was to sleep that night. At Rugby, before Arnold's time, the boy's fath
would be paying an additional four guineas a term to secure him a single be
and both there and elsewhere the sharing of beds was commonplace an
accepted. Before it was divided up into cubicles in 1863, conditions for th
Collegers living in Long Chamber at Eton were notorious. A witness to th
Clarendon Commission recalled his time there in the 1820s:

On entering that renowned dormitory a scene of indescribable confusion
greeted me. It was nearly dark, and there were no lights except a few tallow
candles carried about here and there by the boys. The floor was covered with
the bedding, each bundle being wrapped in a coarse horse-rug, far inferior
to what would now be used in a gentleman's stable. This was intended to
serve as a counterpane. The noise and hooting of nearly fifty boys, each trying
to identify his scanty stock of bedding, combined with the shouts of the elder
boys calling their fags, gave me a foretaste of my future lot.

It would not be long before the new boy became personally acquainted wi
the fagging system, but there were other terrors to be faced first, he w

likely to undergo some rite of initiation. How he coped could have significant consequences for the way he was subsequently treated. Language serves a purpose of identifying members of a group, and the new boy might be given a limited period to learn the *argot* of his school, before being tested in it. Thus, at Winchester he would have to learn the difference between 'bibling' (a flogging of six strokes) and the less painful 'scrubbing' (a flogging of a mere four strokes). He would also have to memorise obscure facts from the school's history, together with such matters as which buttons on his coat he must or must not do up. Some ordeal was likely to be his lot. At Rugby this took the form of 'Lamb Singing'. New boys were required to stand on a table and sing a song of their choosing. This was harmless enough, but if – for whatever reason – he aroused the displeasure of his judges, he was made to drink a brimmer of muddy water mixed with salt. Boys forced to do this could be ill for days. At Winchester in the 1840s, the initiate might be given a pair of 'tin gloves', supposedly so that he would be better equipped to make his fag-master's toast. A red-hot stick was taken from the fire and was drawn across the victim's knuckles down to his wrist, with similar lines being drawn across them. He was left with a grid of blisters.

At Marlborough small boys had their ears pierced with pins or even pocket knives, or were suspended in sheets over the banisters of an upper corridor. Tossing in a blanket was ubiquitous, and not without dire consequences. At Eton in 1832, Rowland Williams, later a controversial Church of England clergyman, suffered injuries that might have proved fatal. Striking his head, he completely scalped, 'as with a tomahawk'. Bullying would continue. Much of it, if committed outside the school and by their

An engraving from R. B. Mansfield, *School Life at Winchester College*, 1870. Mansfield, who was at Winchester between 1835 and 1840, described the practice of 'toefitying', whereby strings were tied around the toes of unsuspecting sleepers. When the cords were pulled, the hapless victims were forced to rise, hopping wildly, from their beds.

A fag toasting muffins. Pastel drawing by Lewis Baumer, from Ian Hay, *The Lighter Side of School Life*, 1914. One of the reasons fags had originally been given such chores as cooking and cleaning was the dearth of domestic servants in the early public schools. Undertaking these tasks also relieved the older boys, who were under the greatest pressure of study.

social inferiors, would undoubtedly have led to charges of criminal assault. But few acts of cruelty could have been more traumatic that those inflicted on the new boy.

Paradoxically, fagging was defended by some as a protection against bullying behaviour, in that the fag acquired a protector. Although fagging entailed some hardships (little time being afforded to fags for eating their own food, and interrupted sleep being amongst them) it is easy to exaggerate the harshness of the system. Robert Blachford Mansfield wrote of his time at Winchester in the 1830s:

> There is more movement and life in such anecdotes [of harsh treatment] than in a relation of the ordinary kindnesses shown by the bigger to the lesser boys; certainly, I have a more lasting general recollection of benefits received than of cruelties suffered.

He argued that fagging was based not on brute force, but on the moral authority of the prefect and respect to the office. Fagging was unknown in the minority of public schools for day boys, and its severity elsewhere varied. At Eton and Harrow it was less highly organised than at some schools; Charterhouse and Winchester had a tradition of strict and onerous fagging, while Westminster was alleged to have led all others in its harsh treatment of fags.

Not surprisingly, critics sometimes likened fagging to slavery. The *Edinburgh Review* in 1830 claimed that fagging in public schools was the only form of slavery that still existed in the British Isles. In August 1847, the *Hampshire Telegraph and Sussex Chronicle* asked, 'Is a course of slavery in the first instance succeeded by the most despotic power, the only way by which the character of our English youth can be formed and prepared for future success?' Many would have

THE FAG :
"SIC VOS NON VOBIS"

Left: A room shared by two brothers at Eton in 1896. The beds fold up against the wall, and are probably set either side of the windows on the right. The room is full of sporting memorabilia, including decorated Procession of Boats hats, acquired new each year for the Fourth of June celebrations.

Below: Boys in their study at Haileybury around the turn of the twentieth century.

The kitchens at Haileybury College, a photograph by the Reverend W. D. Fenning, a housemaster in the early twentieth century. Although servants were few in number in the early nineteenth century, the schools eventually became significant direct or indirect employers of labour in their neighbourhoods.

answered in the affirmative. If it was the task of the public schools to produce leaders, those whose lot in life would be to give orders, then they first needed to learn to obey orders, and fagging ensured that they learned this lesson. But the circumstances of the newspaper's question needs drawing out. The impetus behind it was the serious illness of a Winchester boy, who suffered heat exhaustion after being required to do cricket fagging on a broiling July day. While regulations laid down a maximum time a boy might be required to 'watch out' for balls that went beyond the boundary, there was considerable peer pressure to exceed the limit.

Boys at Westminster School jostle each other at the window of the tuck shop in this photograph, taken c.1910.

At Harrow, compulsory cricket fagging was instituted in 1853 by the Harrow Philathletic Club, a group of boys given specific authority by Dr Vaughan to organise sport at the school. This was a landmark in the introduction of compulsory games. Marlborough and Harrow vie with each other as to which was the first to make participation in games compulsory for all pupils. In both schools the motivation was a reaction against ill discipline. Christopher Wordsworth, Vaughan's predecessor at Harrow, had been a great athlete whilst a boy at Winchester, being the only one at the college who could run 9 miles in an hour, over hilly country. A keen cricketer, he had caught out for a duck Henry Manning, the future Cardinal, in a match against Harrow. Yet, as Headmaster there he did little to encourage games, and lawlessness flourished. In Wordsworth's time it was in stone-throwing that Harrow boys showed their greatest prowess, and many animals (including tradesmen's ponies) lost an eye or were otherwise injured. Vaughan, on the other hand, was no sportsman; yet it was he who made games compulsory. His great innovation (Arnoldian that he was) was to make the monitors (prefects) his agents in encouraging games,

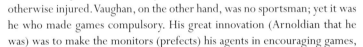

Above: The Eton and Harrow Match at Lord's, from *The Sphere,* 20 July 1901. This match equalled Ascot and the Henley Regatta in the social calendar. In 1910, 15,000 people attended.

Left: The Charterhouse school fire brigade was formed in 1879, seven years after the move to Godalming. Rural isolation of schools had drawbacks as well as advantages. This photograph shows the 'firemen' in 1891.

Above: Montem, at Eton, was an occasion when boys dressed in exotic costumes and went to points around the college (especially Salt Hill, at Slough) demanding salt money from passers by. Very similar in spirit to a contemporary university rag week, the event raised around £1,000, which was intended to finance the Captain of Collegers at university. It was abolished in 1847.

Top right: Squirrel hunting was a popular sport at Marlborough in the early years of the college. As well as catapults, the boys used 'squalers' – lumps of lead the size of a pear attached to a cane handle about 18 inches long. These weapons were probably more deadly than the saloon pistols that some boys used. The engraving dates from 1893.

Bottom right: A House Match at Harrow School, painted by Arthur Garratt, c.1913.

and they became *ex-officio* members of the Harrow Philathletic Club. Cotton, at Marlborough, relied on masters, and when making appointments to his staff he paid as much attention to sporting as to scholastic accomplishments. In June 1853, he issued a 'Circular to Parents' in which he declared that games were to be included as part of the formal curriculum of the school. He, too, wished to cut down on a general lawlessness that pervaded his school. His wife later wrote, 'a civilised out-of-door life in the form of cricket, football, and wholesome sports took the place of poaching, rat hunting and poultry stealing'. Such activities had been common in most schools in earlier years.

Before these changes were introduced, boys had been largely left to themselves in their free time, and they organised their own recreation, either solitary, or in conjunction with their companions. Field sports of all descriptions were popular, and packs of hounds were kept at a number of places. As is the way with boys, many of these activities were rough and tough. The flattened nose that was such a feature of the novelist William Makepeace Thackeray was the result of his having had it broken in a fight at Charterhouse in the 1820s. He was lucky: at Eton in 1825, the brother of Lord Shaftesbury died after a fight lasting two and a half hours. Endurance, or 'bottom', was much lauded, and demonstrated 'manliness'. Even the sports that the boys organised for themselves encouraged toughness. At Harrow in the early nineteenth century, football was played on the gravel courtyard that surrounded the school, the goals being separated by the building. The scarred hands and faces that resulted were considered honourable stigmata. (But not, perhaps, by George Butler, the Headmaster, who considered football a game 'only fit for butcher boys'.) Navvies might have been the comparison made at Rugby, for 'navvies' was the name given to the iron-tipped football boots that were used there, to the detriment of countless shins.

A 'scrummage' during a football game at Rugby. Engraving from the *Illustrated London News*, 10 December 1845. The myth of William Webb Ellis picking up the ball and running with it in 1823, thus 'inventing' the game, seems to have been a later attempt by Rugby School to re-establish its proprietorship.

The Eton Wall Game, shown in a late-nineteenth-century engraving. The game is first recorded in 1766, and had evolved into what is its essential modern form by the late 1840s. The rules are arcane; it is played nowhere else; and the last goal at the big St Andrew's Day game was scored in 1909.

The move towards organised and compulsory games in the latter part of the nineteenth century represented a shift in the character of public school education, which some historians have seen as seismic. The change was marked by the rise of a cult of athleticism, which was defined by W. D. Smith, a historian of sport, as 'the exaltation and disproportionate regard for games which often resulted in the denigration of academic work and in anti-intellectualism' (quoted in J. A. Mangan's book, *see* Further Reading). The training of character had long been a priority of public schools, but in the years after the Clarendon Commission the driving force seems to have shifted from the chapel to the

A late-nineteenth-century engraving of the coxswain of one of the boats taking part in the Fourth of June 'Procession of Boats' at Eton. This celebration commemorated the birthday of George III, who had a great affection for Eton. These days the event takes place on the Wednesday before the first weekend in June.

Above: The words of the *Eton Boating Song* were written by William Johnson Cory, a distinguished master at the College. The music was composed by Captain Algernon Drummond. This most famous of all public school songs inspired imitations, including the *Eton Boating Song Waltz* composed by Karl Kaps c.1895.

Left: Entrance to the playing fields at Eton (*The Boy's Own Paper*, 1886). It now seems firmly established that the Duke of Wellington never did remark that 'the Battle of Waterloo was won on the playing fields of Eton'. (The claim was made by the Count de Montalembert in 1855, three years after the Duke's death.)

Left: John Farmer (1835–1901) was a music teacher at Harrow, and composed many songs, with words often written by masters, especially E. E. Bowen. School songs played an important part in consolidating group cohesion, and nowhere were they more popular than at Harrow. In 1872 Farmer wrote *Forty Years On*, one of the best-known public school songs, in which the chorus echoes the cries of the football field.

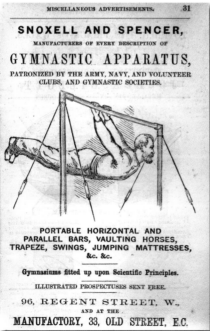

playing field. Gentlemanly conduct a sportsmanship became intertwined. Boys learn to 'play the game', and cheating or po sportsmanship was definitely 'not cricket'. A ne 'athletocracy' came to prevail, which display its less attractive side in the 'blood' with sartorial privileges and his swaggering mann At Harrow, bloods enjoyed the privilege strolling down the middle of the road along t High Street, arm in arm and dressed in the finery. And they continued to do so until t motor car put a stop to the practice!

How can we generalise about the life of t Victorian and Edwardian public schoolboy? T truth, of course, is that we cannot. All institutio change over time, and it would be absurd suppose that the public school of 1837, say, w identical to that of 1901 or 1914. Nor were t schools clones, of one another. Each had individual characteristics, and each boy individual personality. Anthony Trollope hated time at Harrow in the 1820s, but he was a boy there, and his father was continually fighti a battle against poverty. He was no happier Winchester, although he had the grace to acc some personal responsibility: 'I suffered horrib I could make no stand against it. I had no frie to whom I could pour out my sorrows. I was b and awkward, and ugly, and, I have no dou skulked about in a most unattractive mann Lewis Carroll (Charles Lutwidge Dodgson) sp a distinguished four years at Rugby in the 1

Top: Talbot Baines Reed (1852–93) was a prolific writer of school stories, many of them serialised in *The Boy's Own Paper*. The paper was produced by th Religious Tract Society, with which the Reed family was closely associated. Reed's most famous school novel was *The Fifth Form at St Dominic's* (1887).

Bottom: An advertisement for gymnastic equipmen from the *Public Schools Calendar*, 1866. Seven years earlier the first gymnasium in a public school was opened at Uppingham, financed by Thring and his assistant masters.

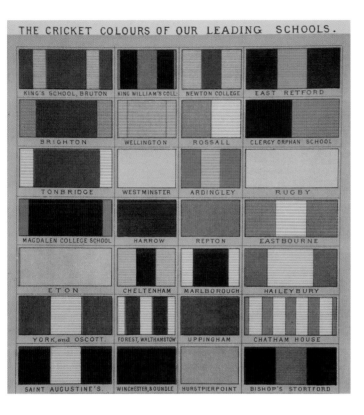

A selection of 'The Cricket Colours of our Leading Schools'. Print given with *The Boy's Own Paper*, June 1884.

1840s, but went on to say, '[no] earthly considerations would induce me to go through my years there again.' Yet many boys enjoyed their time at school and could truthfully say that they were the happiest days of their lives.

A new speech room for Harrow School, designed by William Burges, was built to commemorate the tercentenary of the school, but was not completed until 1877. A speech day of *c.* 1890 is depicted in this painting by an unknown artist.

PUBLIC SCHOOLS
IN AN IMPERIAL AGE

IN *THE HILL*, Horace Annesley Vachell's 1905 novel about Harrow School, one of the characters, 'Caterpillar' Egerton, the dandy son of a Guards officer, explains to his chum, 'At Harrow and Eton, one is licked into shape for the big things: diplomacy, politics, the services. One is taught manners, what?' To manners, he might have added leadership. Victorian and Edwardian public schools possessed a great advantage when it came to initiating boys into an elite culture; they were closed institutions. Boys were set apart during term-time, often in schools occupying remote rural sites, and away from the weakening influence of mothers and other women. Here, they were prepared for a life which, for many of them, would be centred around all-male institutions: the university, the armed forces, the Church, Parliament, the Civil and Diplomatic Services, the City, and the clubs where they took their recreation. Rupert Wilkinson has argued that in many respects the public school can be seen to have performed initiation rights not dissimilar to those of boys in tribal societies. They are taken off by themselves, they endure hardships, they learn signs by which they can identify each other, and they return as men – either warriors or leaders. They can support each other. The ex-public schoolboy is a member of a community marked by the 'old school tie'. In the wide world, he has the support of a network of like-minded men.

At the turn of the twentieth century, the world could hardly have been wider for the Briton, especially the public school man. One fifth of the inhabitants of the globe were subject to the Crown. This vast Empire had to be governed, and it was to the public schools that the nation looked. Edward Mack described the Victorian public school as 'primarily a mint for the coining of Empire builders'. Sir Ralph Furse (Eton and Balliol), a senior civil servant in the Colonial Office, who came to have responsibility for recruitment, said of public schoolboys, 'We could not have run the show without them. In England, universities train the mind; the public schools train character and teach leadership.' In his study of *The English Gentleman*, Philip Mason, educated at Sedbergh, and a former member of the Indian Civil Service, wrote:

Opposite:
Two faces of Britain's imperial history. These contemporary Indian figures represent, on the right, independent India's first prime minister, Jawaharlal Nehru, who was a pupil at Harrow between 1905 and 1907, before proceeding to Trinity College, Cambridge. On the left is another likely old boy of a public school – the British colonial administrator.

Cartoon from *Punch*, 20 March 1929. The old school tie, which enabled former members of a particular school to identify each other, could also deceive, either intentionally or unintentionally. (Hurst Park, West Molesey, was a racecourse and sports complex, with a private membership of over 1,600 when it opened in 1890. It closed in 1962.)

Old Etonian (*getting glimpse of famous tie*). "PARDON ME, SIR, BUT WHEN WERE YOU AT ETON?"
Old Hurst Parkian. "LAST JUNE—WINDSOR RACES."

'Taking thought for the future'. *Punch* cartoon, 13 March 1886.

Pretty Cousin: And what do you think of doing after leaving Harrow?
Tommy: Oh, I shall go into the Indian Civil Service.
Pretty Cousin: Do you think you'll like India then?
Tommy: Oh, it's not that. But, you know, in the Indian Civil a fellow's widow gets such a good pension!

TAKING THOUGHT FOR THE FUTURE.

Above: St John's College, Agra, was established in 1850, to provide secondary education on public school lines for Indian students. The first principal was Thomas Valpy French, an Old Rugbeian, who later became first Bishop of Lahore. From 1873, Haileybury financed a 'Haileybury Master' at the College, which is now affiliated to Agra University.

A man…might find himself at the age of thirty in charge of a million people or an area of five thousand square miles, where he administered justice, kept the peace, and in general played the squire, exercising – ideally – the virtues proper to a ruler, courage, justice and mercy, listening to every petitioner, standing up for his people against higher authority…

Schoolboy portrait of Rudyard Kipling (1865–1936). Kipling was born in Bombay (now Mumbai), India. In 1878 he was sent to the United Services College, at Westward Ho! in north Devon. At first unhappy there, he later thrived, and wrote a fictional account of his experiences in *Stalky & Co* (1899).

Some schools had a particular orientation towards the Empire. Haileybury, when it was founded in 1862, took over buildings near Hertford originally forming the East India Company College, and absorbed many of its traditions. Cheltenham's foreign language department enjoyed a building larger than that devoted to classics, where boys could learn Sanskrit and Hindustani.

Not all former public schoolboys who went out to the colonies did so as administrators. Some went as merchants (often in the family business), as farmers, or as army officers. It is difficult to estimate how many former public schoolboys emigrated in the nineteenth century, for only steerage passengers were required to give full information. Cabin passengers were treated much more casually. Canada was a destination of choice, and by 1913 probably around 40 per cent of higher class passengers went there. Most of these ended up in western Canada, a movement that constituted one of the

key factors in directing the development of the Canadian West on paths s
different from its American counterpart. The *Calgary Herald* observed i
November 1884 (as quoted by Patrick Dunae):

> Calgary is a western town, but is not a western town in the ancient
> sense of the word. It is peopled by native Canadians and
> Englishmen…citizens who own religion and respect law. The rough
> and festive cowboy of Texas…has no counterpart here.

The proportion of public schoolboys going overseas was higher i
the new foundations than in the Great Schools. Marlborough ser
18 per cent of its graduates abroad in the early 1890s; Clifton sen
just under 20 per cent at around the same time. Uppingham an
Haileybury were sending as many as 30 per cent by the mid-1890s
Even those boys who came from a landed or farmin
background in Britain needed to acquire new skills to succeed i
farming in the colonies, and colleges sprang up, both at home an
in the host countries, to give them the skills they would need i
the new environment. New socia
attitudes were required too, i
order to integrate into the les
deferential societies into which the
settled. To maintain a love for th
mother country with a loyalty t
the land of adoption required grea
sensitivity. At the time of the Boe
War, many young Englishmen wh

Top left: Between 1887 and 1900, over
700 young men, most of them from
public schools, passed through the
Colonial College at Hollesley Bay, the
majority ending up in western Canada
As the college song ran, 'There's a
wonderful College at Hollesley Bay,
where Colonists blossom and bloom
into day.'

Left: Sergeant Richard Jones of the
Harrow School Rifle Corps, winner
of the Spencer Cup at the annual
Wimbledon Meetings of 1865–6.
Harrow's Rifle Corps was formed in
1859, the year that saw the birth of the
rifle volunteer movement, as a respons
to a perceived French threat. Engraving
from *The Boy's Own Volume*, 1866.

Colonel Fred Burnaby (1842–85), soldier, adventurer and traveller, embodied many of the qualities for which the public schools were praised. He attended several schools, including Harrow (1855–7). With a height of 6 feet 4 inches, he was reputed to be the strongest man in the army, excelling in gymnastics, weight-lifting, fencing and boxing. (National Portrait Gallery)

had settled in Canada enlisted in Lord Strathcona's Horse, and similar units raised in Australia and New Zealand. Whenever a 'Trooper' or a 'Private' is found on a school war memorial, the chances are that this is a man true to the democratic spirit of his new home.

Moving as are all war memorials, few can be more poignant than those to be found in public schools. Sometimes they are to be found in the school chapel, sometimes housed in a separate building of their own. They remind us of the contributions the public schools made to Victoria's never-ending little wars, to her major wars (such as those in the Crimea and in South Africa), and, most telling of all, to the First World War. Some schools had a particularly strong military tradition, including Wellington, Haileybury, Cheltenham, and the United Services College. Many schools had a Rifle Corps, or its successor the Officers' Training Corps, launched as part of the Haldane army reforms in 1908. Rifle Corps had their origin amidst growing fears of French intransigence in the later 1850s. Rossall claims to be the first school to have started a Corps, on 1 February 1860. Eton, Harrow, Rugby, Marlborough and Winchester all had Corps by the end of the year. To those who see the spread of Rifle Corps as a sign of growing militarism in the public schools, it has to be said that not all took the innovation seriously, but regarded it as an opportunity for a bit of field day fun. The overwhelming view is that until at least 1900 the various school Corps were remarkably ineffective from any military point of view. They met with serious opposition from the games lobby, who resented the time taken away from sports

Right: The Haileybury lines at the annual public schools' camp, ready for the General's inspection, 1893.

Below: Rupert Brooke (1887–1915) was educated at Rugby, where his father was a housemaster. In September 1914, he was commissioned in the Royal Naval Division. His poem *The Soldier* (1914) has been described as probably the best-known sonnet published in English in the twentieth century.

practice. The Headmaster of Westminster declared in 1907 that the school ha a Corps, but it was ineffective as it was 'officered in the main by boys who a not very good at games, and consequently they are not so much respected'.

When war broke out in 1914, there was an immediate response. On August 1914, Lord Kitchener called for 100,000 volunteers. They soon cam forward – but a body of men that size required about 3,500 officers. At fir the army continued to insist that he who aspired to the Queen's commissio should be both 'an officer and a gentleman', and gentlemen came from on place only. (By 1916, it was necessary to take as officers those who would b 'temporary gentlemen' for the duration of the war.) The pressing need w for junior officers, and they poured from the public schools. For some, was like transferring to another school. John Nettleton, who w commissioned in the Artists' Rifles, wrote, 'One had to learn a new set rules and, ridiculous though they might be, they were really no mor ridiculous than the rules one had learned to live with at one's last schoo Such was the social divide of that time that public school recruits were average 5 inches taller than their working class contemporaries. They stoo head and shoulders above most of them; they led from the front; and the died in their thousands. Eton lost 1,157, from a school where the average ro at the time was 1,000. Twenty per cent of their dead had left school betwee 1914 and 1917. Marlborough lost 733; Wellington, 699; Cheltenham, 67 Harrow, 600. The generation that would have led Britain through th troubled 1920s and 1930s was decimated.

UNIVERSITY & PUBLIC SCHOOLS BRIGADE

5000 MEN AT ONCE

The Old Public School and University Men's Committee makes an urgent appeal to their fellow Public School and University men

to at once enlist in these battalions, thus upholding the glorious traditions of their Public Schools & Universities.

TERMS OF SERVICE.

Age on enlistment 19 to 35, ex-soldiers up to 45. and certain ex-non-commissioned officers up to 50. Height 5 ft. 3 in. and upwards. Chest 34 in. at least. Must be medically fit.

General Service for the War.

Men enlisting for the duration of the War will be discharged with all convenient speed at the conclusion of the War

PAY AT ARMY RATES.

and all married men or widowers with children will be accepted. and will draw separation allowance under Army Conditions.

HOW TO JOIN.

Men wishing to join should apply at once, personally, to the Public Schools & Universities Force. 66. Victoria Street. Westminster, London. S.W., or the nearest Recruiting Office of this Force.

GOD SAVE THE KING!

Above: The boyish face of Captain Thomas Colyer-Fergusson, at Harrow from 1909 to 1914. Commissioned into the Northamptonshire Regiment, he died three years later after an attack near Ypres. One of thousands of former public school pupils, he received the Victoria Cross at the age of twenty-one: 'a first-rate officer, a thorough sportsman, and the cheeriest of companions.'

Above: Recruiting poster for the University and Public Schools Brigade, which eventually became the 18th to 21st Battalions of the Royal Fusiliers. 5,000 young men enlisted within ten days, but by the time a training camp was completed at Epsom a quarter had left to take commissions in other regiments.

Right: The public school 'sporting spirit' is exemplified by Captain Wilfred ('Billie') Nevill, who attended Dover College between 1908 and 1913. In May 1916, he purchased a number of footballs while on leave, taking them back with him to the front. On the first day of the Battle of the Somme, he kicked off a football, having offered a prize for the first platoon to reach the German lines. Nevill was shot in the head and killed.

The Magnet 2ᴰ

Billy Bunter's Own Paper

OH, "WAT-ER" SURPRISE for MOSSOO!

No. 1,636. Vol. LV.   EVERY SATURDAY.   Week Ending June 24th, 1939

PUBLIC SCHOOLS AND THE WIDER WORLD

G RAVE THOUGH THE IMPACT of the First World War was on the public schools, it cannot easily be described as a watershed, in the sense that things before and after 1914 were essentially different. The schools went on and continued to flourish, no less so than in our own day (although, in many cases, with the limited admission of girls). New schools in the old mould continued to be founded, such as Stowe, opened in 1923 in a restored eighteenth-century mansion near Buckingham, and including amongst its alumni Sir Richard Branson and the actor David Niven. Schools in a newer mould were also established, including Gordonstoun (1934), which retained the character-building ethos of the Victorian and Edwardian public school while laying great emphasis on rugged outdoor education. Both Prince Charles and his father, the Duke of Edinburgh, studied there, and the school's founder, Dr Kurt Hahn, was instrumental in the setting up of the Outward Bound movement and the Duke of Edinburgh Award Scheme. These initiatives help to spread public school virtues of independence, leadership and service to a very wide social group, as did the Boy Scout movement.

There were other means by which the influence of the nineteenth-century public school spread. Countless boys from the middle and working classes in the late nineteenth century and first half of the twentieth were introduced to public school ideas through comics. However stereotyped their stories may have been, they nevertheless gave their readers access to values that were often missing in their own schools. Foremost amongst the comics of this genre were *The Magnet* and *The Gem*, which were the principal vehicles for a remarkable writer, Frank Richards (whose real name was Charles Hamilton). In the course of a writing career from 1909 to 1961, Richards is estimated to have written between sixty and seventy million words. Many of his stories related to the mythical Greyfriars School, and its anti-hero, Billy Bunter. Robert Roberts was a working-class boy, living in Salford before the First World War, and in his book *The Classic Slum* he sets out eloquently the importance of these school stories to lads like him:

Opposite:
A late issue of *The Magnet*, which ran from 1908 to 1940. After its demise, the exploits of Billy Bunter and his chums at Greyfriars School were kept alive in a series of books, while five series of television adaptations were broadcast between 1952 and 1961.

Many of the trappings and much of the ethos of the Edwardian public school were taken over by the state grammar schools established by the 1902 Education Act. This photograph, taken in 1914, shows Welldon, the cock house at the Harrow County School for Boys, founded in 1911. The master is gowned, and two boys wear Eton collars. 'Virtus Non Stemma' was the school motto – 'Worth Not Birth'!

The standards of conduct observed by Harry Wharton and his friends at Greyfriars set social norms to which school boys and some young teenagers strove spasmodically to conform. Fights – ideally, at least – took place according to Greyfriars rules: no striking an opponent when he was down, no kicking, in fact no weapon but the manly fist. Through the Old School we learned to admire guts, integrity, tradition; we derided the glutton, the American and the French. We looked with contempt upon the sneak and the thief.... With nothing in our own school that called for love or allegiance, Greyfriars became for some of us our true Alma Mater, to whom we felt bound by a dreamlike loyalty.... Over the years these simple tales conditioned the thought of a whole generation of boys. The public school ethos, distorted into myth and sold among us weekly in penny numbers, for good or ill, set ideals and standards.

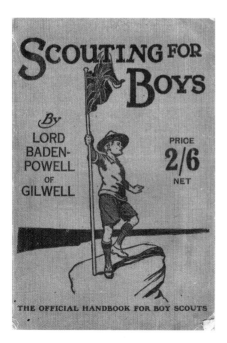

Robert Baden-Powell (1857–1941), the author of *Scouting for Boys*, first published in parts in 1908, entered Charterhouse in 1870 as a 'gownboy' on the foundation. Through scouting he hoped to offer some of those character-building experiences that were perceived to be enjoyed by public schoolboys.

FURTHER READING

Chandos, John. *Boys Together: English Public Schools, 1800–1864.* Yale, 2007.

Copley, Terence. *Black Tom – Arnold of Rugby: The Myth and the Man.* Continuum, 2003.

Dunae, Patrick. *Gentleman Emigrants from the British Public Schools to the Canadian Frontier.* Douglas & McIntyre, Vancouver/Toronto, 1981.

Farmer, J. A. *The Public Schools Wordbook. A Contribution to a Historical Glossary of Words, Phrases, and Turns of Expression Obsolete and in Present Use.* 1900. Reprinted, Kessinger Publishing, 2007.

Fraser, George MacDonald. *The World of the Public School.* Weidenfeld, 1977.

Gathorne-Hardy, Jonathan. *The Public School Phenomenon.* Penguin, 1979.

Hollis, Christopher. *Eton: A History.* Hollis & Carter, 1960.

Honey, J. R. de S. *Tom Brown's Universe.* Millington, 1977.

Hughes, Thomas. *Tom Brown's Schooldays.* New edition, Wordsworth, 1993.

Hurst, Steve. *The Public Schools Battalion in the Great War.* Pen & Sword Books, 2007.

Kipling, Rudyard; edited by Isabel Quigley. *The Complete Stalky & Co.* Oxford, 2009.

Mangan, J. A. *Athleticism in the Victorian and Edwardian Public School.* Cambridge University Press, 1981.

Mansfield, Robert Blachford. *School Life at Winchester College.* 1866, reprinted BiblioBazaar, 2009.

McCrum, Michael. *Thomas Arnold: Headmaster.* Oxford University Press, 1989.

Newsome, David. *Godliness & Good Learning.* John Murray, 1981.

Ogilvie, Vivian. *The English Public School.* Batsford, 1957.

Parker, Patrick. *The Old Lie: The Great War and the Public School Ethos.* Constable, 1987.

Percival, Alicia. *Very Superior Men.* Charles Knight, 1973.

Richards, Jeffrey. *Happiest Days: The Public Schools in English Fiction.* Manchester University Press, 1988.

Seaborne, Malcolm. *The English School: Its Architecture and Organization 1370–1870.* Routledge & Kegan Paul, 1971.

Simon, Brian and Bradley, John (Eds). *The Victorian Public School.* Gill and MacMillan, 1975.

Strachey, Lytton. *Eminent Victorians.* 1918; new edition Oxford, 2009.

Tames, Richard. *The Victorian and Edwardian Sportsman.* Shire, 2007.

Tyerman, Christopher. *A History of Harrow School, 1324–1991.* Oxford, 2000.

Vachell, H. A. *The Hill.* 1905, reprinted BiblioBazaar, 2009.

Wilkinson, Rupert. *The Prefects. British Leadership and the Public School Tradition.* Oxford, 1964.

INDEX